Advanced Options

Trading Strategies

Advanced strategies for

Expert Traders

JAMES DOWNEY

Table of Contents

Introduction

You probably have a good idea of what a share or stock of a company is. In the stock exchange, many things can go on. You will notice that there are going to be many high profiles shares that trade in huge volumes. These also may have some derivatives that are associated with them. A product is a contract that can occur between at least two parties. Sometimes more, the contract will derive its value from an underlying security, such as an index or a stock.

The most-traded derivatives that you can find on the stock market will be options and futures. We will not spend much time on ends in this guidebook. However, they are often easier to understand than alternatives. Yet, they usually have less flexibility and will carry more risk with them.

On the other hand, an option will be a type of contract, one that is sold by one party to another, giving the buyer the right, but not the obligation, to either sell or purchase an underlying stock at a predetermined price. Usually, expiration date or time comes with these options, and the buyer must decide what to do with it in that time frame. They can also choose to work with the underlying asset at any time before the expiration date occurs.

These options cannot exist indefinitely, and each of them has this expiry date. The option buyer will have the right to exercise their buyer at the expiry date or use it before the expiry point. So, when would you want to use an option rather than relying on stocks?

One option is when you know that the underlying option's price may go up in the future. You can purchase the opportunity now, and then when the price does go up, you can exercise your right to buy that stock at the lower price and then sell it to make a profit.

An excellent example of this is when a land developer is waiting to hear if there will be some new regulations put in place on land. If the rules or zoning rules go into effect, the land price will go up. The land developer may enter an options contract with the owner of the land. This gives them the right, but not the requirement, to purchase the ground by the end of the expiry date that the two parties agreed upon. The land developer will have to put some money down as an incentive to the landowner to do the contract.

If the regulations do go through, then the land developer will agree to purchase the land at a reduced price. Their down payment will go towards the amount that they now owe. They never pay more than what the contract stated, no matter how much the land may be worth at the purchase time. The land developer can now make homes in that area and sell them for a good profit because they got such a good deal.

There is some risk involved in this, however. In the example above, if the regulations do not go through, the land developer may decide not to purchase the land. They do not have to make the purchase, but they will have to forfeit the down payment that they made earlier, so there is some monetary loss in the situation.

Types of options

There will be two different types of options that you can work with when it comes to options. There will be call options. These will give the buyer the right to purchase the contract's underlying security at a fixed price. This would be like the example that we talked about above. The put options include options that give the buyer the right to sell the underlying security at a fixed price.

The biggest thing to remember here is that when working with the call option, the buyer of this option can only start to profit from that option if the value of the underlying stock or underlying index goes up. But in the other case with the put option, the buyer of the option can only start to profit when the value of the underlying stock or index goes down.

The benefits and the negatives of working with options

We have spent a bit of time looking at options and what they are all about. There will also be many strategies that you can use when you decide to get into this kind of market, and we will talk about them more as we go. But at this point, you may be wondering why a trader would be willing to start in the options market at all. It often seems more complicated than other forms of investing. A new options trading investor may wonder if the risk is worth the profits in the long run?

There are several reasons why people would choose to work in the options market as their investment choice. First, an investor can profit on changes that occur in an asset's price on the market without ever having to put money up to purchase that equity. They have to pay a premium on that, but they do not have to pay the asset's full price to enter the market. The tip that needs to be paid will come in at a fraction of the cost of what the investor would pay if they bought that asset outright. This can help them leverage their account more to get into a more significant trade without having much capital to start with. Another benefit is that when an investor buys an option instead of just purchasing equity, they can earn more per dollar that they invested compared to what they can do on the traditional stock market. This means that you have more potential profits than you would with conventional financing. But keep in mind that this also means there is more potential for losses with this trading.

Except when selling uncovered puts or calls, the risk that comes with options trading is going to be limited. When you purchase the option, the risk you take on will be limited to the amount of premium you were paying for the opportunity, no matter how much the stock's price moves against the strike price you set. With all these benefits, it is a wonder why everyone does not decide to join the options trading market and use this as their investment tool to make much money. Like all the other investment types that you may try, options do have some main characteristics that will make a few investors turn away and look for other opportunities.

Options are a well-recognized term in the field of trading. Often people assume Options trading is a hard concept to grasp, but it is not so. With the right direction, Options trading can be a handy tool for investors. Bonds, Exchange-traded funds, mutual funds, and stocks are significant classes that form investors' assets. Another asset class is Options. With the right handling and informed guidance, Options can prove to be useful even where other types of assets fail.

As the name suggests, Options are a form of investment that provides us several options. Options can be purchased in the same way as other assets and thus also carry similar risks. It is well known that none of the investments are risk-free. It is suggested that the risks associated with Options are calculated before the trade is done.

Options are associated with derivatives. Derivatives are often paired with risky performance. In the words of Warren Buffett, products are a weapon of mass destruction. The term "derivative" here refers to the derivation of an object's price from another thing. Options are also a form of derivatives under financial securities.

With correct knowledge of the working of options and proper usage of this knowledge in the market, one can steer the odds in their favor. There is no strict way to implement choices; each investor can implement the options in the way they think would benefit them the most. Speculation can take a person a long way in the trading market. Even if an investor does not use options directly, they should still know the possibilities they might invest in might use these options. Chances are a trending tool heavily implemented in MNCs.

Fear can be one of the most dangerous weapons that we use against ourselves. It holds us back from the things we want and makes us push away the things that we need. If you let fear control your life, you will never really oversee any of your thoughts or emotions. Fear can make us nervous, grumpy, and even sick. Almost as bad as this, it can make us lose a ton of money.

Those going into options trading need to make sure that they do not fear holding them back. Though you must be cautious, you should understand that you cannot be too afraid of making a move you might trust. Know the difference between being smart and safe and blinded by worry.

Looking at the Analysis

It is essential to understand how to perform a proper technical analysis to determine the value of a particular option and make sure you do not scare yourself away with any specific number. You might see a dip in a chart, or a price projection lower than you hoped, immediately becoming fearful and avoiding a particular option. Remember not to let yourself get too afraid of all the things you might encounter on any given trading chart. You might see scary projections that show a stock crashing, or maybe you know that it is projected to decrease by half.

Make sure before you trust a specific trading chart that you understand how it was developed. Someone that was not sure what they were doing might have created the display, or there has a chance that it was even dramatized as a method of convincing others not to invest. Always check sources, and if something is particularly concerning or confusing, do not be afraid to run your analysis as well.

You should only base your purchases on concrete facts, never just something you heard from your friend's boyfriend's sister's ex-broker. While they might have the legitimate inside scoop, they could also be completely misunderstanding something they heard. Before you go fearfully selling all your investments from the whisper of a stranger, make sure you do your research and make an educated guess.

Business
Trading
Lorem ipsum dolor sit amet
consectetuer adipiscing elit, sed diam
nonummy nibh euismod tincidunt ut

Advanced Options Trading Strategies

Long Straddle

In a long straddle, you'll simultaneously buy a put and call for the same underlying stock. You're also going to want the same strike price and expiration date. This technique is something that can be utilized with a highly volatile stock. That way, you have the possibility of profiting no matter which way the stock moves. Before we see how this works, let's step back for a second and recall how we determine whether a deal will be profitable.

We are looking at this from the buyer's perspective.

In a call option, you're going to profit when the stock exceeds the strike price. However, you must remember to include the premium in your calculation. If you think a store will go higher than $54, but you're paying a $1 dividend per share, then you will have to invest in a call option that has a strike price of at least $55.

It's the same game in a put option, but you're hoping the stock will go below the strike price. So, for our new scenario of buying a call and a put at the same strike price and expiration date, we will accept a put with a strike price of $55. For simplicity, we will stay with a $1 premium.

Now you need to know the net premium, which will be the sum of the tip from the call option + the bonus from the put option, in this case, $2.

You can get a profit when one of two conditions is met:

Price of underlying stock > (Strike price of call + Net Premium). In our example, you will profit when the amount of the underlying stock is higher than $55 + $2 = $57.

Price of underlying stock < (Strike price of put – Net Premium). Using our example, you'll see a profit when the underlying stock's cost is less than $55- $2 = $53.

The maximum loss will occur when the contract expires with the underlying trading at the strike price. In that case, both contracts expire, and you're out the premiums paid for both options.

A long straddle has two break-even points. These are:

Lower break-even point: Strike price – Net premium

Upper break-even point: Strike price + Net premium

Remember you buy both options with the same strike price and expiration date.

Let's look at a simple example. A stock is trading at $100 a share in May. The investor buys a call with a strike price of $200 that expires on the third Friday in June for $100. The investor also buys a put with a strike price of $200 that passes on the third Friday of June for $100.

The net premium is $100 + $100 = $200.

Now suppose that on the expiry date, the stock is trading at $300. The put expires as worthless since the underlying stock price is far above the put's strike price. However, the investor's call option expires in the money with an intrinsic value of 100 x ($300 - $200) = $10,000. Less the premium, the investor has made $9,800.

On the other hand, suppose that the stock drops in value, and on the expiry, is trading at $50. This time, the call option expires as worthless. The investor can buy 100 shares for $50 each for a total cost of $5,000. Now he can sell them to exercise the put option at $200 a share, so he nets $20,000 - $5,000 - $200 = $14,800.

This is a fictitious example, so whether the numbers are realistic or not isn't the point – the point is that the investor will profit no matter what happens to the stock price.

Example:

Long Straddle

Current Stock Price	Risk-free Rate	Option Style
100	1 %	European ▼

Save

Buy / Sell	Quantity	Call / Put / Stock	Strike	Days to Expiry	Volatility, %	Premium	Debit / Credit
Buy ▼	1	Call ▼	100	365	30	12.3683	-12.3683 ✖
Buy ▼	1	Put ▼	100	365	30	11.3733	-11.3733 ✖
Total							-23.7415

Strangle

The term strangle is an adaptation of the straddle. In this case, you also simultaneously buy a call option and a put option. However, instead of buying them at the same strike price, you buy them at different strike prices. For this type of strategy, you will buy slightly out-of-money options. This is used when you think that the underlying stock will undergo significant volatility in the short term. You will achieve a profit with strangling when one of two conditions are met:

Price of underlying stock > (strike price of call + Net Premium paid) or

Price of underlying stock < (strike price of put – Net premium paid)

Usually, the strike price of the put is set at a lower value. Profit is determined by one of two possibilities:

Profit = Price of underlying stock – strike price of call – net premium

Profit = Strike price of put– the price of underlying stock – net premium

Bear Spread

A bear spread is profitable when the underlying stock price declines. Like the above strategies, a bear spread involves the simultaneous purchase of more than one option; however, you buy two options of the same type in a bear spread.

Bull Spread

A bull spread is designed to profit when the underlying security price has a modest price increase. You can do a bull spread using either call or put options.

Married Puts

A married put is an insurance policy like that we described earlier. You buy a stock and a put option at the same time to protect yourself against possible losses from the store.

Cash Secured Puts

In a cash-secured put, you secure the possible stock purchase by having money in your brokerage account to cover the purchase. This will allow you to purchase stock at a discount, provided you have enough money in your account actually to buy the stock. In short, you write a put option and set aside the cash to purchase the stock. Cash secured put is done when you are bullish on the underlying stock but believe it will undergo a temporary downturn.

Rolling

Rolling a trade means that you simultaneously close out your existing positions and open new ones based on the same underlying stock. When moving a job, you can change the strike price, the contract's duration, or both. You can roll forward, which means extending the expiration date for the option.

A roll-up means that you increase the strike price when you open the new contract. A roll-up is used on a call option when you believe the underlying stock will increase in price. When you are trading put options, you use a roll down. In that case, you close your choice and reopen it with the same underlying stock but with a lower strike price. A higher strike price means that the new position will be cheaper. When rolling, you're going out in time to the deadline. When moving a call, you're hoping that the stock will rise in price. In this case, you're rolling to an out-of-the-money position. The cost of the new call will drop. With a put, the opposite occurs, and the price of the unknown put will increase.

Short strangle option example:

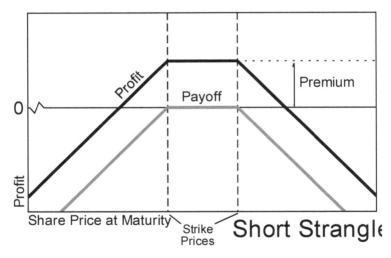

How to Find Stock for Trades

There are thousands of equities available for a trader to choose from. Day traders have no limit on the type of stocks they can trade; you can sell on virtually any store of your choice. With all these available choices, it may seem like a difficult task to know the right stock to add to your watch list. This takes us to the first step in day trading, which knows what to trade.

Here are some tips that will help you to choose the best stocks for maximum profits:

High Volatility and Liquidity in Day Trading

Liquidity in financial markets refers to how one can quickly buy or sell an asset in the market. It can also mean the impact that trading has on the price of a security. It is easier to day trade liquid stocks than other stocks; they are even more discounted, making them cheaper.

Liquid stocks are more significant in volume because one can purchase and sell more substantial stock quantities without significantly affecting the price. Because day trading strategies depend on accurate timing and speed, much work makes it easier for traders to get in and out of trades. Depth is also significant. It shows you the liquidity level of stocks at different price levels below or above the current market offer and bid.

Also, corporations with higher market capitalizations have more liquid equities than those with lower market caps because it is easier to find sellers and buyers for these big corporations' stocks.

Stocks that have more volatility also follow the day trading strategies. A reserve is considered volatile if the corporation that owns it experiences more adjustment in its cash flow. Uncertainty in the financial market creates a significant opportunity for day trading. Online financial services like Google Finance or Yahoo Finance regularly list highly volatile and liquid stocks during the day. This information is also available on other online broker sites.

Consider Your Position

The stocks you decide to go for have to align with your goals and personal situation because there is no one-size-fits-all financial market. You have to consider your capital, risk appetite, and the investment you will take on. Let's not forget the role of research in all these. Your best bet is to read up on different companies' financials, study the market, consider the sectors that best reflect your values, personality, and personal needs, and remember to begin early. You need to be familiar with the market openings and time yourself to follow these openings. While day trading, ensure not to get emotionally attached to a particular stock. Don't forget that you are looking at patterns to know when best to exit or enter to minimize your losses and increase your profit. While you do not have to stay glued to your screen, you still need to know the earning season and what the economic calendar looks like. This will help you to pick the best stocks for day trading.

Social Media

This industry is also another attractive target for day trading. There are several online media companies like Facebook and LinkedIn that have high trading volumes for their stocks. Several debates have been on these social media companies' capability to convert their massive user bases into a sustainable income stream. Although stock prices, in theory, represent the discounted cash flow of the companies that issued them, the recent valuations also look at the earning potential of these companies. Based on this, some analysts think this has led to higher stock valuation than the fundamentals suggested. Regardless, social media is still a popular stock for day trading.

Financial Services

Financial services industries also offer great stocks for day trading. For example, Bank of America is one of the most highly traded stocks per trading session. If you are looking for company stock to day trade, supplies from Bank of America should be among your top consideration, despite the increased skepticism that the banking system faces. The trading volume for Bank of America is high, which makes it a liquid stock. This also applies to Morgan Stanley, Citigroup, JP Morgan & Chase, and Wells Fargo. They all have uncertain industrial conditions and high trading volumes.

Going Outside Your Geographical Boundary

When trading in the financial market, you must diversify your portfolio. Look at stocks listed in other exchanges like the London Stock Exchange (LSE) or Hong Kong's Hang Seng. Extending your portfolio outside your boundary will grant you access to potentially cheaper alternatives as well as foreign stocks.

Medium to high instability

A day trader needs to understand the price movement to be able to make money. As a day trader, you can choose to go for stocks that typically move a lot in percentage terms or dollar terms. These two terms usually yield different results. Stocks that typically move 3% and above every day have consistently significant intraday moves to trade. This also applies to stores that carry above $1.50 each day.

Group followers

Although some traders specialize in contrarian plays, most traders will instead go for equities that move in line with their index and sector group. This means that when the sector or index ticks upward, individual stocks' prices will also increase. This is crucial if the trader desires to trade the weakest or strongest stocks every day. Suppose a trader will instead go to the same store every day. In that case, it is advisable to focus on that stock and worry less about whether it corresponds with any other thing.

Entry and Exit Strategies

After you must have picked the best stocks in the world, your strategies will determine if you will profit from them or not. There are several available day trading strategies, but you need to stick to specific guidelines and look out for individual intraday trading signals to increase your chances of success.

Below, I will talk about 5 of these guidelines:

Trade Weak Stocks in a Downtrend and Strong Stocks in an Uptrend

In a bid to pick the best stocks for day trading, most traders prefer to look at EFTs or equities with at least a moderate to high connection with the NASDAQ or S&P 500 indexes and then separate the strong stocks from the weak ones. This creates an opportunity for the day trader to profit as the healthy store can go 2% up when the index moves 1% up. The more a stock moves, the more opportunity for the day trader.

As market futures/ indexes move higher, traders should purchase stocks with more aggressive upward movement than futures. Even if the lots pull back, it will have little or no impact/ pull back on a healthy supply. These are the stocks you should trade in an uptrend as they provide more profit potential when the market goes higher.

When the futures or indexes drop, it becomes profitable to short sell those stocks that fall more than the market. The ETFs and supplies that are weaker or stronger than the market may change each day; however, specific sectors may be relatively weak or strong for weeks at a time. When looking for a stock to trade, always go for the strong one. This same rule applies to short trades as well. As a short seller, you should isolate EFTs or stocks that are weaker so that when prices fall, you will have greater chances of having profited by being in EFTs or stores that fail the most.

Trade Only with the current intraday Trend

The trading market always moves in waves, and it's your job as a trader to ride these waves. When there is an uptrend, your focus should be on taking long positions while taking short classes whenever there is a downtrend. We have already established that intraday trends do not go on forever but, you can carry out one or more trades before a reversal occurs. When there is a shift with the dominant trend, you should begin to trade with the new trend. It may be challenging to isolate the movement. However, you can find useful and straightforward entry and stop-loss strategies from Trend lines.

Take your time.

Wait for the Pullback trend lines to provide visual guides that show where price waves will start and end. So, when choosing stocks to day trade, you can use a trend line for early entry into the next price wave. When you want to enter a long position, be patient, and wait for the price to move down towards the trend line and then move back higher before you buy. Before an upward trend line can appear, a price low before a higher price low needs to happen. A line is drawn to connect the two points and then extends to the right. This same principle applies when short selling. Be patient for the price to move up to the downward-slope trend line, and once the stock starts to move back down, you can then make your entry.

Take your profits regularly

As a day trader, you have limited time to make profits, and for this reason, you need to spend very little time in trades that are moving in the wrong direction or losing money. Let me show you two simple guidelines that you can use to take profits when trading with trends:

In a short position or downtrend, take your profits slightly below or at the former price low in the current trend.

In a long position or uptrend, take your profits slightly above or at the former price high in the current trend.

Do not play when the market stalls

The market may not always trend. The intraday trends may reverse so often that it becomes hard to establish an overriding direction. If there are no significant lows and highs, ensure the intraday movements are large enough to increase the chances of profits and reduce the risks of loss. For instance, if you are risking $0.15 per share, the EFT or stock should move enough to give you a minimum of $0.20 - $0.25 profit using the guidelines stated above. When the price is not trending (moving in a range), move to a range-bound trading technique. During a degree, you will no longer have an angled line but rather a horizontal line. However, the general concept still applies: purchase only when the price goes to the lower flat area (support) and then begins to move higher. Short sell once you notice that the price has reached the upper horizontal line (resistance) and begins to go lower again.

Your buying strategy should be to exit close to the top of the range but not strictly at the top. Your shorting plan should be to go in the lower part of the content but not precisely at the bottom. The chances of making gains should be more than the risk of loss. Place a stop loss just above the most current high before entry on a short signal or just below the most recent low before access on a buy signal.

How to Trade Options

First is that you have to think of your investment objective. You do not go there in the trading aimlessly because you will lose much money. Remember that options require that intelligent speculation because you are dealing with future gains. You have to establish realistic and measurable values that you expect. Such goals will give you a way to go and the route to follow. You may plan which type of optional trading you want. That is where you want the put-off option or the call option. Moreover, do you want to speculate on the underlying asset's performance or hedge out their risks?

You have to examine the risks and the returns that the assets may bring you. Your biggest aim is always to harness sizeable gains while reducing the risks. You think that there are risks in the present and decide to buy them in the future. Or you, with the put-up option, predicting that the shares will fall in the price and award others the right to protect their expected depreciation. You have to be tolerant, optimistic, and persistent in your tasks. If you are a risk-taker, this is the right avenue for you. If you sense a volatile market, exploit that opportunity to gain much.

Identify the different events of the market of the sector you are trading. Those events will institute the volatility of the occurrence. You can either experience a drift or a rise in the market. Those events can be grouped in two ways: the market-wide, and the other is the stock specif. The market-wide are like those government jurisdictions that affect the economy of the whole sector. For example, the government banning or subsidizing some products. In the stock-specific one, they include issues like product launches and many others.

You have to derive the right strategies after knowing the stocks to trade and the returns you desire. These are distinctive tactics that you will apply to harness many gains. You must be that intelligent speculator who will read the patterns and realize the peak points and market volatility. Moreover, a device some strategies like selling a call option against the stock. That is a tactic where you exercise a covered call approach on the security that you already own. You must sell the cover calls against your shares to identify the profitable spot. The other strategy is using the bullish or bearish method for the call option and put option, respectively. Always buy options on significant stock platforms where you anticipate a substantial fallout of the industry's top players.

Decide on the right parameter to facilitate your marketing. These are like the variables you will use to make a successful trading. Remember that this trade requires one to know the trend, price analysis, and many other types.

Options Trading for Income

It has already been determined that options are bought and sold just like other financial commodities. Options are contracts that are entered into between a buyer and a seller. As a trader, you can buy votes at the options market through a broker. You can also approach writers and request options to be written concerning an underlying stock you are interested in.

The contracts entered into having a predetermined price as well as an expiration period. This period ranges from 3 months to about a year though this varies for various reasons. Therefore, a seller and buyer will agree on the terms of an options contract before entering into one.

The Options Markets

There are different options markets available. Options can be based on a variety of securities. These range from commodities like gold or grain to stocks such as Bank of America shares and even currencies like the US dollar and the British Pound. Different traders have different needs and hence the variations when it comes to options contracts.

Reasons Why Traders Choose Options

There are also different reasons why traders, and others, choose to deal in options rather than other financial instruments. For starters, options can be used for hedging purposes. For instance, a person may survey the market or receive information that their stocks will plummet in the coming months. Now, if the person holds substantial amounts of stock, then the losses could be significant. But hedging provides a form of security.

Another reason why traders prefer trading options is because of the enormous profit possibilities. Compared to other securities, options can be a source of immense wealth. Several billionaires made their fortunes trading options. There are also numerous multi-millionaires and other superbly wealthy individuals whose fortunes were all made trading options. This is why more and more traders are opting for this approach. You also get to profit from options regardless of the market trends. This means you can make money when the markets trend upwards when there is a decline, even when there are zero movements.

Options Fundamentals

Options type: There are generally two types of options that you can sell or buy. These are called opportunities and put options.

Strike Price: The strike price is also known as the exercise price. This is the price you will sell or buy the underlying stock should you choose to exercise your options.

Expiration Date: The options contract is not indefinite and has an expiration date. The expiration date referred to the date when the contract entered becomes void or expires.

Premium: This term refers to the price you pay for the option. This price is charged per share, which means it will depend on the number of shares you sign up for. Premium has different components to it. These are the intrinsic value and time value of an option.

Intrinsic Value: This is the value of an option and refers to the difference between the underlying stock's strike price and its current market price.

Time value: The time value of a share refers to the amount of time available before an option's contract expires. The time value decreases as the expiry date approaches.

Time decay is the term used to express the approach of the expiration date. As this time decay progresses, the time value of an option decreases. Time decay is also commonly referred to as "theta." This time is derived from the pricing model that was used to calculate it. Time is precious to investors hence the importance of time decay.

Other Terminology used in Options Trading

Listed options: A listed option is an option that qualifies for trading at a national trading platform like the Chicago Board Options Exchange, CBOE. A listed option generally represents 100 shares of a particular stock. Such an option with 100 shares is also referred to as one contract. Each contract has fixed expiration dates and strike prices.

In-the-money: A call option is said to be in-the-money when the share price exceeds the strike price. On the other hand, a put option is said to be in-the-money anytime the share price falls below the strike price.

The price, or total cost, of any option is referred to as the premium. It is affected by many factors, including volatility, time value, strike price, and stock price.

Contract names: Options contracts do have names or options symbols similar to ticker symbols for stocks.

Ask price: This is the asking price that a seller will accept to trade the option. Basically, should you wish to purchase options, and then this would be the premium you would pay.

Volume: This refers to the total number of contracts that get traded in one day

Change: This refers to the difference in price from the previous to the current trading period. Sometimes change is expressed in terms of percentage.

Volatility: Volatility merely measures a stock's price swing measured between the low and high prices each day. For a long time, volatility has been calculated using past data.

IV, also known as implied volatility, measures the likelihood that a market considers a stock will experience a significant price swing. Specific tools are used to measure some of these parameters. One of these is Vega. Vega is a pricing model that calculates the theoretical effect of a single point change in implied volatility.

When the implied volatility is high, option prices will be increased due to the potential upside for the options contract. It is good to keep in mind that volatility measurements are only estimates and never accurate. They are mostly predictions on the expected change of an option's price.

Employee stock option: While these are not readily available for all traders, they are a call option. Plenty of listed companies offer stock options to their treasured and talented staff members, especially management, to retain them for a long time.

Employee stock options are very similar to ordinary stock options. A holder receives the right, but not the obligation, to purchase stocks at a specific price and within a stipulated period. However, the contract only exists between the company owners or board and an employee. Others cannot trade or exchange it at the options stock markets.

This is different, however, if the options are listed. A listed option represents a contract between two other parties. This contract is entirely unrelated to the company and easily be traded at the markets.

Terms Describing an Option's Value

We do not describe an option's performance as up, down, or level. This kind of description is not sufficient. Instead, we can see the definite version in one of three distinct ways.

In the money: An option that has intrinsic value is said to be in-the-money. Anytime a stock's price in the stock market and the strike price favor the contract owner; the option contract is said to be in the money. Essentially, it is beneficial to the call option owner when the stock price is greater than the strike price. On the other hand, a put option is said to be in the money when the stock's cost is less than the strike price.

Out of the money: An option is said to be out of the money when there is absolutely no monetary gain expected in exercising it. This means it is a lot less lucrative or financially viable to sell stocks and shares at the strike price than it would in the general securities market. Therefore, we say that a call option is out of the money if the strike price is higher than the stock price. On the other hand, a put option is said to be out of the money anytime that the stock price is increased than the strike price.

At the money: Sometimes, the strike price is just about equal to the stock price. In such a situation, we say that the option is at the capital.

Options Seller and Buyer Terms

There are special terms used to refer to options traders. In other situations, we'd refer to the traders as buyers and sellers. However, when it comes to options trading, a more technical term is used.

Writer: The term writer refers to an investor who holds an options contract and is selling it. When the writer sells the option, they will receive a premium from the buyer. The buyer will be buying the right to buy a specific amount of shares at a strike price.

Holder: A holder is an investor seeking to purchase an options contract. A call options holder will buy an options contract and gain the right to buy the underlying stock under stipulated terms. A put holder possesses all the rights to sell the underlying stock.

A holder and a writer are generally on opposite sides of an options transaction. One writes an option while the other signs up to it. However, the main difference between these two is the kind of losses they are exposed to.

Holders sign up to get the right to purchase or sell shares but without obligation. The contract that they sign up grants them the choice of if and when to exercise their rights. Over time, if the option becomes out-of-the-money, they have the freedom to abandon the contract and let it expire. In such an instance, they will only lose the premium paid to set up the options contract.

On the other hand, things are a little different. For instance, writers lack this kind of flexibility. Suppose a call options holder decides to exercise their right. In that case, the writer is obligated to accept the order and execute it by selling the stock at the current strike price. Should the writer not own all the shares in a contract, they will have to purchase these at current market rates and sell to the holder at the strike price. If there are any losses to be incurred, the writer is obligated to take on them. Since the risks are pretty high for writers, it is recommended that beginners confine themselves only to buy stock options until they gather sufficient experience over the years.

Options are another asset class. If applied correctly, they will offer numerous benefits that all other assets on their own cannot. For instance, you can use options to hedge against adverse outcomes like a declining stock market or falling oil prices. You can use options to generate recurrent income and speculative purposes like wagering on a stock's movement.

Options Strategies

Strangles and Straddles

This type of strategy is used when the stock is expected to make a large pricing move, but you don't know how it will move. It involves buying a call and put an option together in a single trade. A strangle consists of setting an abounding range for the expected stock movement, using different strike prices for the put and call option. A lower strike price is used for the put option, while a higher strike price is used for the call option. The break-even price is the break-even price for the call option if the stock rises or the break-even price for the put option if the stock drops.

For example, if the share price was $100, but it was expected to make a big move, you could set up a strangle with a $105 call option and a $95 put option. If the stock prices fail to move either above the call option strike price or below the put option strike price, you will lose money on the trade. The maximum possible loss is the cost of buying the options.

The strategy is considered neutral because it will make profits if the stock moves up (powerfully) or down (powerfully). You will invest in this type of strategy when you expect a large move in the store, so, for example, many traders buy before an earnings call. Most earnings call result in the stock's significant price movements. However, you aren't sure which direction it will move before the market.

The strike prices selected for the call and put option will be out of the money. Both options will have the same expiration date.

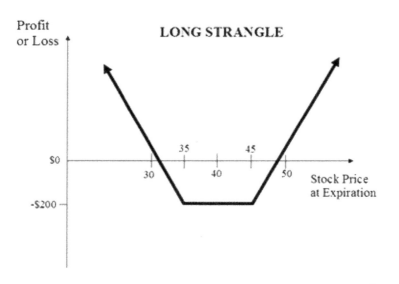

The maximum profit on the upside is theoretically unlimited. However, it will depend on how far the stock price moves above the call option's strike. If that happens, the put option expires worthless, and your profit selling the call option less the cost of buying the put option is your net profit. If the stock price drops, the maximum gain will occur in the doubtful case that it fell to zero, less the call option cost. If the stock price moves to any level below the put option's break-even price, you can earn a profit.

A straddle is used for the same purpose, but in this case, we set the strike prices of the call and put the option to the same value, and both options will have the same expiration date. With a straddle, you want the stock price to move off the strike price used in either direction.

Iron Condor

An iron condor is one of the most popular options strategies. This is an income-producing strategy. An iron condor is sold for a net credit (keep this in mind, there is much misinformation about iron condors). An iron condor is sold using a call credit spread and a put credit spread, all in the same trade. The two options with inner strike prices will be sold. So, for example, suppose that a stock is trading at $200 a share. You could sell a call option with a strike price of $205 and buy a call option with a strike price of $210. Simultaneously, you would sell a put option with a $195 strike price and buy a put option with a $190 strike price.

As long as the stock price stays in between the inner strike prices – ranging between $195 and $205 in our example – you will make a profit. An iron condor is used when you expect the stock price will not change very much over the options' lifetime. All options used in an iron condor have the same expiration date.

To pick your strike prices, determine where support and resistance are. You want to set the strike price of the put option you sell slightly above the support price and set the call option's strike price a little bit below the resistance price. Then select the outer strike prices slightly above the resistance price level for the purchased call option and below the support price level for the purchased put option.

Many traders make a full-time living strictly selling iron condors. The chart has the following form.

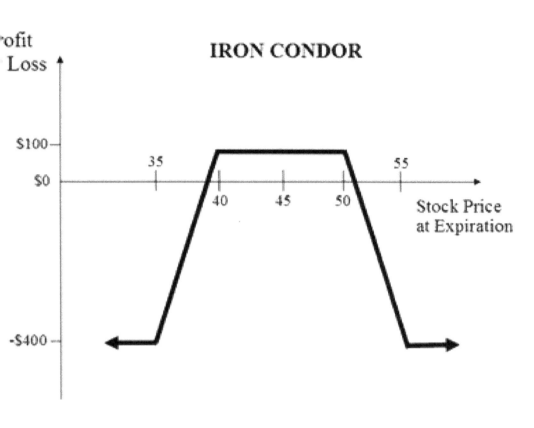

You will receive a net credit for the call credit spread and a net credit for the put credit spread. The total credit received is your maximum profit. If the stock remains in between the inner strike prices, this is when you will earn profits.

One advantage of the iron condor is that losses are also capped. Should the stock move to the upside, the maximum loss is the difference in the two call options' strike prices. Should the stock move downward, the maximum loss is the difference between the put options' strike prices. Using our example here would be a $5 loss (per share – total $500) if the stock moved below $190 or above $210.

Iron Butterfly

An iron butterfly is a less popular way to set this up since it creates a narrow range for the stock. In the case of an iron butterfly, you set your inner strike prices the same. For example, using a stock trading at $200, we could sell a call option and a put option with a $200 strike price, buy a call option with a $205 strike price and buy a put option with a $195 strike price. Losses will be incurred if the stock price goes above the $205 strike of the upper call or below the $195 strike of the put.

Equity Collar

This is a strategy used to hedge risk. It is used on a long stock position that you have, and large traders use this. So, to use this strategy, you would have a large number of shares of some stock.

If you are uncertain about the stock's direction that you own, you could set up an equity collar to hedge your risk with put and call options. You set it up by buying an equal number of put and call options with strike prices above the share price for the call options and strike prices below the share price for put options. The options will all have the same expiration date. If the share price moves above the call strike price, you will earn profits on the call options, and the put options will expire worthlessly. If the stock price moves below the put options, the call options will expire worthlessly. You can exercise the put options and sell your stock at a higher price than the market price or sell the put options for a profit and keep your inventory.

Short Gut

A short gut is a less popular options strategy that involves selling a call and a put option simultaneously. You sell the two options with the same expiration month but not necessarily the same expiration date. First, you sell a call option at a specific strike price, and then you sell a put option with a higher strike price. Maximum losses are uncapped if the stock price moves in either direction, so you hope the stock price will stay the same. Maximum profit is equal to the premiums received from selling the options. This is a little-used strategy, and you must be a level 4 options trader to use it. You must have enough cash in your account to cover selling the two options (cash as collateral).

Long Gut

A long gut involves buying a call option and buying a put option with a higher strike price. In this case, you hope to profit from the stock moving in either direction, so it is someone analogous to a strangle. However, you are doing it with the strike prices of the call and put reversed. If the stock price moves up, you will make money from the market but lose money on the put; if the strike price moves down, you will make money on the put and lose on the call.

Synthetic Strategies

Synthetic strategies are obscure and rarely used by small traders. To make a synthetic put, you must have a large margin account. To set it up, you will short the stock, so you will borrow shares of stock from the broker and sell them on the market, hoping to repurchase them at a lower price. Then you will buy a call option on the same stock. If the stock price rises, you will make a profit on the call option to help offset the loss of repurchase the shares at a higher price (if you borrow shares from the broker, you have to repurchase them and return them to the broker at some point). If the stock price drops as expected, you will lose money on the call option, which will expire worthlessly. However, you will make the expected profit from shorting the stock. You can repurchase it at the lower share price, return the shares to the broker, and then the profit from doing that less the cost of the call option is your net profit. So, this involves shorting stock using a call option as insurance.

Options Trading and the Individual Investor

Suppose you want to fully understand and predict the entry and exit points in the market. In that case, a technical understanding analysis should be your priority. Fundamental analysis is all about making decisions based on industry trends, valuation, and revenue. On the other hand, technical analysis is about volume and price from historical data. In this method, investors implement behavioral economics and statistical analysis to bridge the gap between market price and intrinsic value.

In technical analysis, there are two different approaches, and you must choose the right one for yourself –

- Top-Down – This approach is more about macroeconomic analysis. This means that this approach is less about individual securities and more about the overall economy. The primary focus will be on the economy. Then the focus will shift to the various sectors and then finally to the companies present in those sectors.

- Bottom-Up – The next one is just the opposite. The investors focus more on individual stocks rather than a macroeconomic analysis. If a particular store seems interesting, this approach will help find the possible entry and exit points in that stock.

How to Get Started with Technical Analysis?

If you are just a beginner, then here are some of the basic steps that you should implement to get started with technical analysis –

- Develop a trading system – This is the first step. It means you have to identify a technical analysis strategy that works for you. For example, if you are a beginner, you might go for the moving average crossover strategy. In this method, you will be keeping track of the two moving averages on any particular stock's changes in price.

- Find the right strategy for your tradable security – Not every system is meant for all deposits. If your tradable securities are options, then you have to find the plan that fits it. Sometimes, the parameter choices also start changing with the protection you choose.

- Choose the right brokerage account – The next step is to choose the correct brokerage account where you will be able to trade the type of security you have chosen. Not every brokerage account gives you the tools needed to perform technical analysis of options. The brokerage account you choose should have proper monitoring and tracking functionality with the technical indicators you need.

Also, you need to make sure that your costs are low so that your profits are not affected.

- Choose an interface to monitor trades – Depending on the strategy you have chosen, the functionality you also need changes. So, select your interface carefully.

  - See whether you need any more applications – Sometimes, you might need other applications to maximize the performance. Some traders prefer trading on the go, so they look for platforms that would give them mobile alerts. If there are any such special requirements, think about whether you need any more applications to support you.

Technical analysis for options trading is slightly different mainly because there is time decay in options. You cannot hold a position for an indefinite period. There is an expiration date for every opportunity before which you will have to leave it. So, some of the common technical indicators used in this case have been explained in the next lines.

Common Technical Indicators for Options

Since options trading is a form of short-term trading, some of the things that you can determine with the help of technical indicators are as follows –

- The direction of the movement

- Range of movement

- Duration of the movement

RSI or Relative Strength Index

This is a momentum indicator. With the help of RSI, you can measure the magnitude of the losses and gains incurred over a specific time and then compare them to find out the change of price movements and speed of activities of security. This will, in turn, help you point out oversold and overbought conditions. The value of RSI is usually between 0-100, and an RSI value indicates overbought levels over 70. Oversold levels are characterized by a value less than 30.

When options are based on individual stocks, the RSI values perform the best compared to indexes. If you want to achieve short-term trading by looking at the RSI value, then options on high-beta liquid stocks are what you should look for.

Bollinger Bands

Bollinger bands are one of the best ways to do so when there is an increase in volatility, these bands increase. Similarly, when there is a decrease in volatility, these bands contract. When the price moves to become close to the upper band, it suggests that the security might have been overbought. On the contrary, when the price moves so that it becomes comparable to the lower band, it indicates that the deposit might be oversold.

You can predict a reversal when you see a price movement outside of these bands. And predicting all of these helps the option traders to position themselves correctly. For example, if you notice a breakout above the top bar, you can initiate a short call or a long put. On the contrary, if there is a breakout below the lower band, it can be predicted as an opportunity for a short put or long call.

You must also not forget that it is the periods of high volatility when you should be looking forward to selling options to make profits because this is when the prices of options are elevated.

Similarly, when there is low volatility, you should consider buying options because the costs of alternatives are a downside.

IMI or Intraday Momentum Index

If you are a high-frequency trader and want to start trading on intraday moves, then the IMI will prove to be an excellent indicator for you. The concepts of RSI and candlesticks are combined in this particular technical indicator. With the help of this strategy, initiating a bullish trade becomes more comfortable. You will be able to spot the possibilities where you can do so in a trending market. Similarly, the technical indicator will also help you initiate a bearish trade in a market by spotting the right possibilities in a downward trending market.

MFI or Money Flow Index

Both the volume and price data are combined in this particular index. That is also why this is sometimes known as volume-weighted RSI. This technical indicator can measure the outflow and the inflow of money into an asset when considered over time (for example, two weeks). This indicator is also an indicator of trading pressure. You will know that particular security has been overbought if the MFI value is above 80. On the other hand, you will understand that specific security is oversold if the MFI value is below 20.

Since MFI depends so much on the volume, it is better suited for trading options solely on stocks and the ones done for a longer time. You can predict a change in the trend if you notice that the stock price and the MFI are moving in opposite directions.

OI or Open Interest

Any unsettled or open contracts in options are indicated by the OI or Open Interest technical indicator. But keep in mind that this technical indicator does not necessarily denote that there will be a specific downtrend or uptrend. You can find out the strength of a particular trend with the help of this technical indicator. You can predict the inflow of new capital when there is an increase in OI. This also indicates that the existing trend is going to sustain. Similarly, you can spot a trend is weakening when the values of OI decrease.

PCR or Put-Call Ratio

With this particular technical indicator's help, you will be able to get an idea of the trading volume by comparing the call options with the put options. If there is a change in the overall market sentiment, it can be predicted by a difference in the value of PCR.

The PCR value is more than one when the number of puts exceeds the number of calls. This means it is a bearish market. Similarly, the PCR value is less than one when the number of calls exceeds the number of puts. This means that it is a bullish market.

Key Differences Between Fundamental Analysis and Technical Analysis

- Suppose you are looking for a more long-term approach in analysis. In that case, it is a fundamental analysis because, with its help, you can figure out which stocks are about to witness a rise in value in the upcoming days. Technical analysis is more of a short-term approach, and that is why it is more relevant for options trading and day trading. In this, you will get to know which stocks can bring you profit if you buy them now and then sell them in the future at a higher price.

- Investing is the main objective of fundamental analysis since it is all about the long-term. But trading objectives form the core of the technical analysis.

- The intrinsic value of a stock is used in fundamental analysis so that profitable stocks can be identified in the long term. The past performance of stocks is taken into account in the case of technical analysis. Its price movement for the future can be predicted from that.

- Both present and past data regarding a stock are considered in the case of fundamental analysis. Only the past data is deemed in the case of technical analysis.

- Financial statements and data are analyzed to make decisions in fundamental analysis. Price movement trends and charts are analyzed to make decisions in the case of technical analysis.

- There are no assumptions when you are performing fundamental analysis. You will have to make several assumptions in technical analysis. For example, you may have to assume that the price will follow a similar trend as it did in the past.

Advantages & Disadvantages

For Fundamental Analysis

Advantages:

- Only sound financial data are used to perform fundamental analysis. Thus, there is no scope of personal bias anywhere.
- You will arrive at a proper recommendation to either buy or sell by using analytical and statistical tools.
- Several long-term trends of demographic, economic, consumer, and technological origin are considered.
- Rigorous financial analysis and accounting pave the way for understanding everything in-depth and leaves room for no mistakes.

Disadvantages:

- When you are considering the financials, some assumptions have to be made. So, I always advise everyone to consider both the worst and best scenarios. There can be unexpected legislative or economic changes at any time.
- The entire process of industry analysis takes up much time, and it is not a cakewalk.

For Technical Analysis –

Advantages:

- You come to know the possible entry and exit points in the trade.
- You get to know how the overall market is performing and judge the prevailing sentiments running.
- When you notice patterns, you can predict directions of movement.

Disadvantages:

- The underlying fundamentals are not taken into consideration while performing technical analysis. And thus, several risks can crop up because of this.
- Sometimes, if your chart is full of too many indicators, then the signals can be confusing.

Transaction

There are many things you need to consider when making transactions in Day Trading, and these are:

Selecting Brokers

When it comes to selecting brokers, you have many options available. There is full service, discount, online, etc. Understanding the differences between them and selecting the ones best suited for your purposes is crucial if you wish to succeed. Many beginners ignore and then receive a rude lesson in the regulations surrounding options trading.

There aren't too many rules to comply with, but they do have significant consequences for your capital and risk strategies.

What broker to use?

Generally speaking, there are two significant varieties of brokers: Discount and full service. A lot of full-service brokers have discount arms these days, so that you will see some overlap. Full service refers to an organization where brokerage is just a part of a larger financial supermarket.

The broker might offer you other investment solutions, estate planning strategies, and so on. They'll also have an in-house research wing that will send you reports to help you trade better. In addition to this, they'll also have phone support if you have any questions or wish to place an order.

Once you develop a good relationship with them, a full-service broker will become an excellent organization to network with.

Every broker loves a profitable customer since it helps with marketing. A full-service broker will have good relationships in the industry, and if you have specific needs, they can put you in touch with the right people.

The price of all this service is you paying higher commissions than average. It is up to you to see whether this is a reasonable price for you to pay. As such, you don't need to sign up with a full-service broker to trade successfully. Order matching is done electronically, so it's not as if a person on the floor can get you a better price these days. Therefore, a full-service house is not going to give you better execution.

Discount brokers, on the other hand, are all about focus. They help you trade, and that is it. At least not intentionally from a business perspective, they will not provide advice, and phone ordering is nonexistent. That doesn't mean customer service is reduced, far from it.

Commissions will be lower as well, far lower than what you can expect to pay at a full-service house. The downside of a discount brokerage is that you're not going to receive any unique product recommendations or solutions outside of your speculative activities. Many people prefer to trade (using a separate account) with the broker they have their retirement accounts with, so everything is kept in-house.

So which one should you choose? Well, if you aim to keep costs as low as possible, then select a discount broker. Only in the case where you're keen on keeping things in one place should you choose a full-service broker. These days, there's no difference between the two options otherwise.

An exception here is if you have a large amount of capital, north of half a million dollars. In such cases, a full-service broker will be cheaper because of their volume-based commission offers. You'll pay the same rate or as close to what a discount broker would charge you, and you get all the additional services. Whatever other amounts you need to invest can be handled by the firm through their business wealth management line.

You must understand a few terms, no matter which broker you choose, so let's look at these now.

Margin

Margin refers to the number of assets you currently hold in your account. Your purchases are cash and positions. As the market value of your classes fluctuates, so does the amount of margin you have. Margin is an important concept to grasp since it is at the core of your risk management discipline.

When you open an account with your broker, you will have a choice to make. You can open either a cash or margin account. To trade options, you have to open a margin account. Briefly, a cash account does not include leverage within it, so all you can change are stocks. There are no account minimums for a cash account, and even if they are, they're pretty minuscule.

A margin account, on the other hand, is subject to very different rules. First, the minimum balances for a margin account are higher. Most brokers will impose a $10,000 minimum, and some will even increase this amount based on your trading style. The account minimum doesn't achieve anything by itself, but it acts as a broker's commission.

The thinking is that with this much money on the line, the person trading will be a bit more serious about it and won't blow it away. If only it worked like that. Anyway, the minimum balance is a hard and fast rule. Another rule you should be aware of is the Pattern Day Trader (PDT) designation.

PDT is a rule that comes directly from the SEC. Anyone who executes four or more orders within five days is classified as a PDT ("Pattern Day Trader," 2019). Once this tag is slapped onto you, your broker will ask you to post at least $25,000 in the margin as a minimum balance. Again, this minimum balance doesn't do anything but the SEC figures that if you do screw up, this gives you enough of a buffer.

Each strategy by itself plays out over a month or more, so once you enter, all you need to do is monitor it, and if you want, you can adjust it. However, if you're going to avoid the PDT, you're limited to entering just three positions per workweek.

My advice is to study the strategies and to start slowly. Trade just one instrument at first and see how it goes and then expand once you gain more confidence. At that point, you'll have enough experience to figure out how much capital you need. Remember that even exiting a position is considered a trade, so PDT doesn't refer to trade entry.

Building up your Watch list

One other aspect of margin you must understand is the margin call. This is a dreaded message for most traders, including institutional ones. The purpose of all risk management is to keep you as far away as possible from this ever happening to you. A margin call is issued when you have inadequate funds in your account to cover its requirements.

Remember that your margin is the combination of the cash you hold plus the value of your positions. If you have $1000 in cash, but your work is currently in a loss of -$900, you'll receive a margin call to post more money to cover the potential loss you're headed for. You'll receive it well in advance. If you don't post more margins, your broker has the right to close out your positions and recover whatever cash they can to stop their risk limits from being triggered.

The threshold beyond which your broker will issue a margin call is called the maintenance margin. Usually, you need to maintain 25% of your initial position value (that is, when you enter a position) as cash in your account. Most brokers have a handy indicator that tells you how close you are to the limit.

The leading cause of margin calls is leverage. With a margin account, you can borrow money from your broker and use that to boost your returns. Let's look at an example: if you trade with $10,000 of your own money and borrow $20,000 from your broker to enter a position, you control $30,000 worth of the work. Let's say this position makes a gain of $10,000 to bring its total value to $40,000.

You've just made a 100% return on this investment (since you invested only $10,000) despite the total return on the position is 33% (10,000/30,000). What happens if you lose $10,000 on the job, however? Well, you just lost 100% despite the position losing only 33%. Leverage is a double-edged sword.

It is far too simplistic to call leverage terrible or good. It is what it is. If you're a beginner, you should not be borrowing money to trade under any circumstances. When you're experienced, you can choose to do so as much as you want. Please note I'm differentiating between the leverage you borrow money and the sort of leverage options you provide.

A single contract gives you control over a larger pie of stock with options, but the option premium still needs to be paid. It is, therefore, cheaper to trade options than the common stock. Suppose you were to borrow money to pay for the option premium. In that case, you're indulging in foolish behavior, and you need to step away.

There's a difference between leverage being inherent within the instrument's structure and using power to increase the amount of something you can buy. The latter should be avoided when you're a beginner.

Execution

A favorite pastime of unsuccessful traders is to complain about execution. Their losses are always the broker's fault, and if it weren't for the greedy brokers, they'd be rolling in the dough, diving in and out of it like Scrooge McDuck. Complaining about your execution will get you nothing. A big reason for these complaints is that most beginner traders don't realize that the price they see on the screen is not the same as what is being traded on the exchange.

We live in an era of high-frequency trading. The markets' smallest measurement of time has gone from seconds to microseconds. Trades are continually pouring in, and the matching engine is always finding suitable sellers for buyers. Given the market's pace, it is essential to understand that it is humanly impossible to figure out an instrument's exact price. Therefore, within your risk management plan, you must make allowance for high volatility times when the fluctuations will be more significant. For now, I want you to understand that just because the price you received was different from what was on screen doesn't mean the broker is incompetent.

How do you identify an incompetent broker? Customer service and the quality of the trading terminal give you access to be the best indicator. Your broker is not in the game to trade against you or fleeces you. So stop blaming your broker and look at your systems instead, assuming the broker passes essential due diligence.

When it comes to placing orders with your broker, you have many options. There are different order types you can remember, and each order has a specific purpose. First off, we have the market order. This is the most straightforward order to understand. When you place a market order, you're telling your broker to fill your entire order at whatever price they can find on the market.

Rules for Successful Trading of Options

To succeed in the world of options trading, you are required to trade by following specific rules and tips. All the information you will find here can help you achieve all you wish to have in trading. Mistakes are meant to be made when you first start with trading. So, let's look at some of the basic rules of options trading and try your best to avoid mistakes.

Having Knowledge About the Time for Improvising the Plan

One of the most critical aspects that are needed for successful trading is having a proper plan. Besides that, you must also take care of one more thing, which is the perfect time for improvising your techniques. There will be several instances when you will have to shift away from the plan. Your emotional aspects might also not work in such cases. To be successful in the world of options trading, you need to have proper knowledge regarding the plan's time when it will be losing its validity. As you create an appropriate strategy for trading, it can help you set up a valid path. But, as you set up the way for yourself, that does not indicate you will be moved by the same way blindly right to the end of the world. Every trader needs to pass through a point of time in their trading career when everything seems to go out of hand. This will ultimately be making the proper plan turn into something utterly useless for that specific situation.

That is why, when you are having the thoughts of designing a new plan, you need to identify all its weak points. As you are the one who is creating all trading plans, you will have proper knowledge when it can fail. The conditions of the trading market will keep on changing. So, what you have planned might work today but will not be the same the other day. Suppose you are trying to keep on following your plan of action that has been predetermined. In that case, even if the market condition gets turned 360-degree, you will be making a big mistake. When you keep on following a fixed plan of action, you are most likely to fail. You will surely need much practice to understand the market scenario. The conditions will keep on changing. But, as you take a small step in the right direction, you can call it to progress. This also consists of being aware of the significant differences between the present situation and the situation tomorrow.

Avoiding Trades That Are Out-of-the-Money

With the help of specific strategies, you can generate some profit by purchasing out-of-the-money call options. But such trades are only a few in numbers and can be treated as exceptions. As you enter the options trading world, you will most likely get attracted like a magnet to out-of-the-money call options. It is very natural. The main reason behind this is that such opportunities are affordable and cheap than the others. But you are also required to keep one thing in mind: the stock market and options market are different from one another. Even when you dedicate all your attention to the underlying security while buying options, that cannot be considered a good strategy. It won't be a great idea if you are willing to purchase low and then sell them out as high as a call option tends to be out-of-the-money; the chances of the same rising again to the required levels before the expiry date is shallow. So, if you are willing to purchase options of this nature, you will be doing nothing but gamble with all that you have.

Preparing the Entry and Exit Plan Before Starting

Trading of options is all about finding out the perfect positions of entry and exit. You are required to learn this thing first in the proper way before you start trading. No matter what kind of techniques you will be using for the adjustment, nothing can rectify a bad entry point. This might even result in you incurring a considerable loss. But there is something more meaningful in options trading than fixing the proper entry and exit points. Do you have any idea what exactly it is? It is the knowledge that you need to exercise the entry and exit points much before you have given in all your capital.

Most of the beginner options traders believe that every trade they will make will bring vast profits. They give in their all for making the best out of the last cent spent by them. If you want to succeed as a trader in the world of options, you cannot start following this idea. When you aim to bring in vast amounts of profits, it can bring in new obstacles to your path. Until and unless you have a proper plan related to trading that can bring in profits, you will perform several trades that can develop small gains. When you fix up your mind to stick to only one specific business as if it is the only one left, you will be doing wrong. It will be resulting in huge losses for you.

So, once you have gained a potential amount of small profits from various trades, there is no need to think about the same again. You are only required to protect all that you have made. Of course, you can ignore this suggestion and keep on trading with your trading plans. It can bring you more potential profits as well. But the fact is that the loss you will be incurring will be much more than the actual gain. You might lose all your profit without even getting the chance to use it properly.

Not Trading for Wealth

If you think of options trading so that the returns you will be getting will be more than 150% or so, it will be better for you if you step back and try to reconsider your position. There are indeed certain investments that can bring in vast amounts of profits. But all the trades that you are going to make will not be the same. Various options traders think that options trading will be making them rich in one night. But, in reality, nothing happens like that.

In case you have opted for options trading to generate wealth, you have made up a wrong notion about the trading of options. Options trading is all about working with the perfect strategy to make sure of daily income flow. As you try to be hungry for grabbing huge profits, there are chances that you will be overseeing the risky aspects. Never forget that options trading is hazardous. If you take one wrong step, all that you have can vanish in a second.

How to Maximize Profits with Options Trading

Now it is time to move on to some of the steps you can take to maximize your profits with options. Options are a great way to earn a profit because they allow you to reduce your exposure and the amount of risk you take on while increasing the number of gains you could make. Some of the tips that you can use to help maximize your profits while options trading includes:

Tip 1: You can profit no matter the market situation

One of the first things that you will notice when working in the options market is that you can benefit from any situation in the market when you work with options. Most of the strategies that work with this investment vehicle are carried out by combining the different option positions. Sometimes, they will even use the underlying part of the stock. You can use either different trading strategies, or work with a few together, to profit no matter what market situation is going on.

When you enter the market with options, you always stand to make a considerable amount of profits while still keeping your risk to a minimum. Ordinary stock trading isn't as reliable, and it comes with a lot more risk. The most crucial aspects of options trading know when you should enter a trade and how you should exit it. Knowing how and when to go will ensure that you keep any losses to a minimum and that you can increase your profits as much as possible.

You will find that options strategies are considered one of the most versatile in the financial market. They will provide investors and traders alike with many profit-making opportunities. There is a limited amount of risk and exposure present. This is one of the main reasons that many investors like to take some time and invest in options instead of other asset choices.

Since you can profit no matter what the market situation is doing, this gives you much freedom when working with options. But it also means that you may have to learn a lot more strategies than usual. You should know at least a few plans for a rising market, for a stagnant market, and a downturn market. This will ensure that you are ready to go no matter which way the market is heading.

While making a profit in any market is a great thing and can open up many new opportunities to make money compared to just investing in the stock market, it does make things a bit trickier to work with. You have to understand where the market is going. You have to know which strategies work for the different market directions. You have to be ready to switch back and forth depending on how the market is doing.

Tip 2: Take advantage of the volatility of options to make a profit

Options have some similarities to stocks, but they are a bit different. And one place you will notice these differences is with the time limit. Stocks can be held for as short of a period or as long as you want, but options have an expiration date. This means that the time you get to do the trade is going to be limited. And as a trader, missing this window will be a costly mistake, one that you need to avoid if at all possible. If this chance is omitted, then it may be a very long time before you see it again.

This is why it is never a good idea to work with a long-term strategy when trying to trade with options. Techniques, such as working with the average down, are seen as bad choices for options trading because you don't get the right time frame to see them happen. Also, make sure that you are careful about margin requirements. Depending on what these are, they could significantly impact the criteria for the number of funds you can invest.

There are also times when multiple factors may affect a favorable price. For instance, the cost of the asset you choose may go up, which is usually seen as a good thing. But it is possible that any of the accruing benefits could be eroded due to other factors, such as volatility, time decay, and dividend payment. These constraints mean that you need to learn how to follow some of the different strategies for profit-taking.

Tip 3: Always set a profit-taking stop loss

The next tip that you should follow is to set up a profit-taking stop loss. You can set up a stop loss at about five percent. This means that you want it to reach a target price of $100 if the trailing target is going to be $95. If the upward trend continues and the price gets to $120, then the trailing mark, assuming the 5 percent from before, will become $114. And it would keep going up from there, with the amount of profit you wish to make in the process.

Now, let's say that the price is going to start to fall. When this happens, you will need to exit and then collect the profits at this level or the trailing target you set. This ensures that you get to enjoy some protection as the price increases, and then you will exit the trade as soon as the price starts to turn around. The thing that you need to remember here is that the stop loss levels should never be too high or too low. If they are too small, you will be kicked out of the market too soon in most cases. But if they are too large, they will make it impossible to enjoy profit-taking.

Tip 4: Sell covered call options against long positions

Selling options Is an income-generating process that is pretty lucrative. Depending on the amount of risk you take and what kinds of trades you decide to do, you could easily take home more than two percent in returns each month. However, this is not the only method you can use to make it rich on the market. You can also go with something that is known as a naked put and sell these. This is similar in the way of trading stocks or shares that you don't own.

When you go through the process of selling a naked put option, you will be able to free up some of your time to do more. Stock trading allows you to have an opportunity to sell stocks of shares that you don't already own, and then you can earn a profit. This will free up your capital, allowing you to invest it or trade with it indefinitely.

To make this method work, it is best to work with stocks that you already understand well or don't mind owning. This way, you know when there are any significant changes to the store, and you can make some changes to the way you invest before the market turns and harms your profits. There is still a level of hedging associated with this options trading method, so you must always be on the lookout for that.

Tip 5: Pick the right strategy

And often, the one that you pick will lead you to find the right options to sell. Some of the options trading strategies are going to work in a downturn, some are going to work the best in an upturn, and some do well when the market is more stagnant. When you pick out a strategy, you will choose the options that fit in with that strategy the best.

With that said, there are a few guidelines that you can learn to follow when it is time to purchase an option for trading. Following these guidelines will make it easier for you to identify the options you should choose to profit from. Some of the policies include:

Determine whether the market is bullish or bearish. Also, make sure that you determine whether you are strongly bullish or just mildly bullish. This can make a difference in how the market is doing and which assets you would like to work with.

Think about how volatile the market is right now and how it could affect your strategy with options trading. Also, you can think about the status of the market at the time. Is the market currently calm, or is there much volatility that shows up? If it is not very high, you should buy the call options based on the underlying stock. These are usually seen as relatively inexpensive.

Consider the strike price and the expiration date of any options you want to trade-in. If you only have a few shares, this may make it the best time to purchase more of the stock or asset. Your overall goal of working with the options trading market is to make as much profit as possible. No one goes into the market, or any investment, with the idea that they want to lose money. But if you follow some of the tips above, you will maximize your profits and see some great results.

Risk Management and Mindset

Quantitative and Qualitative

Risk per Trade

More than anything else, it is your risk per trade that determines your success. The common wisdom is not to risk more than two percent of your capital per transaction, and in the case of options trading, this is correct. Directional trading requires you to risk far less than this to be successful.

The accurate measure of a profitable trader is how consistent they are in risking the same percentage of their account on every trade. Many beginners get on a winning streak at times and then start playing loose with this, only to be hit by a significant loss that wipes out all their prior gains.

A school of thought proposes that risking a fixed amount per trade, instead of a fixed percentage, is a better model. Now, you must understand that entire books can be written on risk management, and I don't have space here to explain statistically why this is a bad idea entirely. Suffice to say that risking the same amount will bring you more significant gains per trade and exaggerate your winning streaks but will do the same to your losses.

Win Percent

The win percentage of your strategy, that is, the number of times you make money, is one-half of an important measure that determines whether you'll make money or not. Usually, thanks to the way we've been brought up and have had UR performances measured in school, we chase the highest win percentages, thinking ninety percent is better than forty. Well, in academia, this is true. However, in the chaotic world of the markets, this is far from the case. Making money on a trade is not about being right. You can be right about the needs and still lose money in the long run. This is best explained after we look at the second half of the equation.

Average Win Percent

Your average win percent is the amount of money you win on average when you make money, expressed as a percentage of your account or a multiple of the amount you risk per trade on average. So, if you risk R per transaction, which might be 2% of your account, and if you make 4% on a win on average, you will make 2R per win.

The average win percent and the win percent together determine whether you'll make money or not. If you win two out of ten trades, a win rate of twenty percent and your average win is 2R; you will not make money. This is because your eight losses will cost you 8R, and your victories will only amount to 4R. This is a net loss of 4R.

However, if you make 5R on average per win, you will make money with a twenty percent win rate. In this case, your losses will add up to 8R as before, but your victories will add up to 10R, giving you an overall profit of 2R. If you risk two percent of your account, this is a profit of 4% over ten trades.

Now, if you manage to take two hundred trades over a year, you'll be making 80% in a year. This is precisely what professional traders do make. It takes an extraordinarily high level of skill to hit such numbers. My point is that your profitability is determined by both numbers, not just a single one.

Strategy Evaluation

This gives us an excellent method of figuring out the profitability of strategies. If a system has a low win percent but a high average win percent, it is perfectly valid to implement it instead of chase plans with high win percentages. For example, if you have the latest described strategy and another one with a 90%-win rate but only a 0.5R average win percent.

Over two hundred trades, the earlier strategy makes 80%, but this strategy, which is correct 90% of the time, will make you 35% over the same number of trades. So, which is the better strategy? The one where you have more losses or the one where you have more wins? Asking which one has more wins or loses is missing the point.

Qualitative Risk

Let's say you settle down in front of your television on the weekend and switch on the TV to catch your favorite game. You're fully prepped and have your TV and assorted accessories set just so. Your friends have come over as well and all in all, it's a great atmosphere. There's only one problem: your team's star athlete, the one on whom the result of the game hinges, has turned up to the game hungover.

Now, it isn't unheard of such things to happen in pro sports, but when it does happen, you can imagine the reaction that follows. The athlete is roundly criticized as a buffoon, rightly so, and the sports media have a field day debating where he's about to be traded to next. We instinctively understand that preparation is the key to success, and turning up hungover is hardly adequate preparation.

Do you seriously think anyone can be successful trading this way? Do you think trading is simply a matter of learning the right strategies and then implementing them with the snap of a finger? This indicates that your mindset is incorrect and that you don't understand what trading risk management involves. Make no mistake; you will need to fully prepare and have your wits about you as you sit down to trade. You cannot afford any distractions like checking your smartphone or trying to wing something at the last minute. It would help if you had an adequate sleep and need to exercise and eat well.

This is why I called the adrenaline-filled, coked-out atmosphere of trading floors in movies unrealistic because it is impossible to trade this way. Many beginners get seduced by this 'devil may care' type of depiction and try to do the same when it comes to their own hard-earned money. This results in a quick wipeout, and the ones who will take their money are the traders who have prepared themselves.

You need to follow a specific mental and physical routine before operating in the markets. Meditation and other mental calming techniques are great ideas and will enable you to see things clearly, as they are. Also, avoid trading when things are not going well for you with your regular life.

Mindset

The biggest hurdle we face is our in-built negativity bias. The negativity bias is a part of our survival mechanism that gives greater priority to harmful things than things that provide us with pleasure. Thus, you are more likely to remember negative experiences than positive ones.

This is precisely why many people chase high win rate systems irrespective of the strategy's overall profit potential. We are so conditioned to think that a high win rate means avoiding lousy performance. We forget to consider how much we make per win on average.

This is also why executing a twenty percent win rate system is difficult and requires a very high degree of skill. A twenty percent win rate implies losing eight out of ten trades. Most people cannot stomach losing two businesses in a row, let alone being able to remain disciplined and absorb fifteen losers in a row (there is a 98% chance you will experience losing fifteen trades in a row if your strategy has a twenty percent win rate). Simply reading that last sentence has probably convinced you that taking the less profitable strategy from the previous part is a good idea, but this negates bias. To trade successfully, you need to build a different mental model when it comes to trading.

The type of thinking that favors a high win rate system is excellent in an ordered set, as an academic one. In such settings, you provide correct answers, and you get rewarded. The market, however, is not called. It is chaotic. There are far too many players, too many trading systems, and motivation ever to be able to make sense of it all.

Thus, you need to think in terms of odds and probabilities. Probabilistic thinking is what separates the professionals from the also-rans. Instead of being a gambler, you need to be the casino. This is an excellent example of how odds work, so let's run with it.

A casino knows the odds of each game on its floor. It knows that game X has odds of sixty percent, or that sixty percent of the time, the house wins, and the gambler loses. Given this information, how does the house make money now? Well, first off, they fix the payout in proportion with the bet size.

The games that pay out a mega jackpot of over a million with low bet sizes usually have miserable odds, sometimes as much as ninety-eight percent stacked against the gambler. The game plays for itself via the number of hands people play. Even if the odd gambler wins the mega jackpot, it doesn't matter since the odds will play out and even themselves out over the long-run, and the house will make its money eventually.

This is why gamblers are plied with free drinks and comped rooms. Everything is set up to get you in a good mood and ignore the fact that you're flushing your money down the toilet and are stacking the odds against you the longer you play. This is why jackpot winners are immediately provided comped rooms and treated like royalty because it is in the casino's best interest to get them to gamble those winnings and increase the house's profits.

Hopefully, you're seeing the parallels with trading strategies now. Why should you care about a single trade? An extensive number matter results since the odds express themselves over a large sample size, not a small one. Thus, even if you do lose fifteen trades in a row, this means you're more likely to win the next one since the odds will even themselves out the longer you participate.

Thus, your primary focus should be on maintaining the odds and the math that goes with it. Changing your risk percent every trade skew the math out of your favor since your average win sizes are now skewed. Your only focus should be to maintain the odds according to your calculations and focus on keeping your capital safe. The longer you keep your money safe, the longer you play, and the more you win.

A lot of us have toxic beliefs about money and becoming successful thanks to deeply ingrained programming. Perhaps we grew up poor or had a scarcity mindset when it comes to money.

Successful traders:

- Understand the odds of their system and know it inside out
- Are consistent with risk management
- Push the limits when it comes to expanding their skills
- Follow a structured and precise training regimen to develop their skills
- Recognize their negativity bias and limiting beliefs and implement techniques to combat this, including:
- Meditation
- Visualization
- Positive Affirmations
- Breathing Techniques
- Are well capitalized and do not seek 'get rich quick' shortcuts
- Practice on paper first before going live
- Protect their capital at all costs
- Do not dream of Ferraris and yachts after a few wins on the trot
- Do not dream of despair and poverty after a few losses
- Do not need the market to validate their self-image
- Set their ego aside and follow their discipline and risk management rules

Conclusion

Thank you for making it to the end. Trading is gradually exploding into a profession. There have been many courses and seminars regularly being conducted on the importance and the techniques of day trading. All these educational materials and methods aim to raise your education level in the field of trading.

The key to master, the art of day trading is maintaining knowledge and discipline. When you are sitting in front of your trading computer screen with your finger on the trigger, you are about to take decisions in split seconds. Your choices can help you rake in thousands of dollars while at the same time, it can strip you of thousands of dollars.

CPSIA information can be obtained
at www.ICGtesting.com
Printed in the USA
BVHW091141060521
606650BV00010B/1372